Thrift Store Knick Knacks Into Giant Cash Stacks

50 Everyday Items You Can Buy Cheap At Thrift Stores And Resell On eBay And Amazon For Huge Profit

Table of Contents

Introduction

Chapter 1: Where to Begin and What to Buy

Chapter 2: Easy to Find Items You Can Make a Profit on

Chapter 3: What Else Should You Look For?

Chapter 4: Even More Items You Can Resell For Good Money

Chapter 5: Unique Items You Never Thought Would Sell

Chapter 6: Some 1980's Items You Can Sell and Make a Profit on

Chapter 7: Some Odd Selling Items That Sell Great

Conclusion

Introduction

I want to thank you and congratulate you for downloading the book, Turning Thrift Store Knick Knacks Into Giant Cash Stacks: 50 Everyday Items You Can Buy Cheap At Thrift Stores And Resell On eBay And Amazon For Huge Profit.

This book contains proven steps and strategies on how to flip thrift store items and sell them for a profit on eBay.

This book is for anyone who wants to learn how they can purchase items from a thrift store and sell them for a profit on eBay and Amazon. All of the items listed in this book are guaranteed sellers. As you learn about the different items you should look for while you are shopping, you are also going to learn great tips and tricks that will help you be successful at flipping the items for huge profit!

You are going to learn about everyday items that are easy to find in any thrift store. You will also learn about generic categories as well as specific items that you should look for. In addition, you will learn how you can find items on your own that may not be listed in this book, but that you will still be able to sell for a profit.

Finally you will learn what you should do in order to make your business a success. By following the advice and tips in this book, you will be well on your way to making big time money reselling thrift store items on eBay and Amazon.

Thanks again for downloading this book, I hope you enjoy it!

© **Copyright 2015 by _____Rick Riley_____ -
All rights reserved.**

This document is geared towards providing exact and reliable information in regards to the topic and issue covered. The publication is sold with the idea that the publisher is not required to render accounting, officially permitted, or otherwise, qualified services. If advice is necessary, legal or professional, a practiced individual in the profession should be ordered.

- From a Declaration of Principles which was accepted and approved equally by a Committee of the American Bar Association and a Committee of Publishers and Associations.

In no way is it legal to reproduce, duplicate, or transmit any part of this document in either electronic means or in printed format. Recording of this publication is strictly prohibited and any storage of this document is not allowed unless with written permission from the publisher. All rights reserved.

The information provided herein is stated to be truthful and consistent, in that any liability, in terms of inattention or otherwise, by any usage or abuse of any policies, processes, or directions contained within is the solitary and utter responsibility of the recipient reader. Under no circumstances will any legal responsibility or blame be held against the publisher for any reparation, damages, or monetary loss due to the information herein, either directly or indirectly.

Respective authors own all copyrights not held by the publisher.

The information herein is offered for informational purposes solely, and is universal as so. The presentation of the information is without contract or any type of guarantee assurance.

The trademarks that are used are without any consent, and the publication of the trademark is without permission or backing by the trademark owner. All trademarks and brands within this book are for clarifying purposes only and are the owned by the owners themselves, not affiliated with this document.

Chapter 1
Where to Begin and What to Buy

Deciding that you are going to start purchasing from thrift stores and reselling on eBay is a great business to get into, but it is just that, a business. Those who are successful at purchasing from thrift stores and reselling on eBay and Amazon can spend 40 to 60 hours a week shopping for and listing their items. They also have to spend time learning about each of their items and what the hottest selling items are.

You see, one day you may be able to get $30 for an item you purchased for $3 and the next day you may not be able to sell that same item at all. It all depends on how many people are selling that specific item on eBay. Throughout this book I am going to teach you which items you should look for while you are searching through thrift shops, as well as give you tips on how to ensure your success at selling on eBay and Amazon.

1. Clothing. Yes you can sell clothing on eBay, but you need to be very careful about the types of clothing you purchase from a thrift store. First you need to make sure there are no stains or snags, you need to check and make sure there are no buttons or zippers missing. The next thing you need to know is that not all clothes will sell on eBay. Watch for big and tall clothes for men, plus size clothing for women, name brand clothing and polo shirts. These are the types of adult clothes that sell the most. Always be on the lookout for vintage mens hawaiian shirts. You want to be looking for loud, vibrant hawaiian shirt designs.

   Childrens clothing also sells very well but it needs to be a recognizable brand. You will not be able to sell childrens no name clothing no matter how great the condition is. Watch for brands like Old Navy or Gymboree when purchasing childrens clothing.

2. College books are also a great thing to keep an eye out for when you are shopping at a thrift store. If you live near a college town you can find tons of these super cheap, post them on eBay or Amazon and make a great profit! You do need to make sure the books are not written in and that they come with any computer software that is needed. Make sure they are in good condition and none of the pages are torn out. Students spend tons of money on these each year and many are turning to purchasing online, so if you can get some before the school year starts chances are you will make a great profit.

3. Keep your eye out for board games the next time you go to a thrift store. If you can find vintage board games that are still in good condition and contain all the pieces for the game you will make a profit off of it. One vintage game I always sell for huge profit is called Crossbows And Catapults.

4. Shoes are one item that many people overlook because they think there is no profit to be made, but if you can find name brand shoes from the 70's you will be able to purchase them for a few dollars and sell them for up to $50. Always buy vintage Converse and Nike shoes if they are in good condition and have a unique design.

5. Old telephones are a great item to keep your eye out for as well. Rotary telephones sell for $1-$2 at a thrift store but you can make $30-$40 dollars on them when you list them on eBay. This is before shipping so you don't have to worry about shipping eating into your profits. All you need to do is make sure that the phones still work. Most thrift stores will have a sticker on items that say 'works'. If your store does not, then simply ask if it has been tested and if they will test it for you.

6. Toys are another item you should watch for. Now I am not saying you should go out and purchase a ton of junk

toys from thrift stores, what I am saying is you should watch for specific toys. I regularly find vintage He-Man and Star Wars toys from the 1980's at garage sales.

One warning I have for you though, you want to look for things that have slid by the workers at the thrift store. When the store knows what they have they will usually place it behind glass. For example, one store I went to had a Raggedy Ann and Andy dolls. They wanted $50 for them, knowing I could only sell them for about $30 a piece, it was not worth it for me to even consider purchasing them. The store knew they had an item that was worth something. If you find yourself in a thrift store wanting to buy something that is a bit out of your price range, but you know you can make a profit on, always ask to talk to the store manager. Many times they have worked the price down for me or I offer to make a package deal with other items. You never know until you ask!

7. Video games are something else you need to keep an out for. I was once wandering through a thrift store and saw a Zelda game for the Game Boy gaming system still in the box for $3. I got it, went home and sold it for $25 before shipping. It is items like this that you want to watch for, things that you will pay little for and that will sell quickly. Any Nintendo games, Game Boy games or even Atari games will sell quickly and for a great profit. The great thing about these is that they are easy to ship as well.

8. Black and white photographs. This is another item that many people over look but sells great on eBay! They are also super easy to ship. Don't ask me why black and white photographs sell so well, I would never be able to answer that. What I do know is that it does not matter who the photograph is of, all that matters is that it is in good condition and that it is an old photograph.

Those eight items are a great place to start when it comes to purchasing items from thrift stores and selling them on eBay and Amazon. My tip for you in this chapter is that you should always keep a smart phone with you so that if you do come across an item that you think may sell quickly on eBay, you will be able to check and see if you are going to be able to make a profit from it. Check to see what the item is currently selling for on eBay and how many people are actually selling the item. If you find an item selling for $30 and you can purchase it for $3, you may want to consider it. However if you find there are 250 people on eBay trying to sell the same item, chances are you will not make a quick profit. This is okay for some people and you have to decide how long you are willing to let the item sit before you want to make profit from it.

Chapter 2
Easy to Find Items You Can Make a Profit on

In this chapter I want to continue giving you lots of items you can find at thrift stores and resell on eBay and Amazon for a profit, but I want to focus on the easier items that you can find.

Those that don't take a lot of searching but can still bring in a profit. When I am looking for an item to sell, I only look for items that I can sell for at least 5 times what I paid for it. Sometimes I will purchase an item that will not sell for that much if it is something I know will sell fast and is easy to ship.

9. Coffee mugs. This is an item that is so easy to find and so many people overlook it. Keep an eye out for any StarBucks mugs, Disney, Looney Toons or Snoopy mugs. You can usually get these for 25 to 50 cents and sell them for $5 to $25 dollars depending on the condition and the brands.

10. Tupperware. I am not talking about plastic ware that you can purchase at the grocery store or dollar store. I am talking about real Tupperware. Even if you only find one piece you are still going to be able to turn a great profit on it. You can purchase a piece of Tupperware at a thrift store for a couple dollars up to $5 and turn around and sell it for $15-$30 dollars depending on the condition and the size.

11. Pig items. This is another one of those items that makes no sense to me and I can't tell you why they sell but anything pig related sells great on eBay. This was an odd find for me. My mother collected pigs, I bought her some when I was at a thrift store and a week later someone had stolen them all off of her porch. I went back and got her more and began thinking, if someone

wanted them so bad they would steal I bet I could sell them. I listed a pig I purchased for $3 and sold it for $32! Keep your eye out for those PIGS!!

12. Old bottles of perfume are another item you can find at thrift stores. When I say old I mean OLD not just used. You need to look for fancy bottles and it does not matter how much of the perfume is left. Of course, the more perfume that is in the bottle, the more you will be able to charge but most people will pay for just the bottle by itself.

13. Artwork. This is an item that is a little harder to ship but it is definitely worth looking into. You can regularly get a large piece of art for $5-$10 dollars and sell it very quickly. Even if the artist is unknown, keep an eye on the frames. Many people will purchase the artwork just so they can get an antic looking frame.

14. Old magazines are a great seller as well and let's face it, thrift stores are full of these. You can usually get them for 5 to 10 cents and depending on the topic sell them for a lot more. You want to make sure that they are in good condition, all the pages are intact and they are not torn. You should look for rare or odd subjects such as flying airplanes or bowling. You do not want to look for magazines such as national geographic or magazines that you can find anywhere.

15. Fur is an item you have to watch for. You will usually find this in the winter and most thrift stores keep fur coats with the regular coats. Many employees are not trained to spot real fur when they get it in and will generally mark the price very cheap. I recently purchased a full length fur coat in perfect condition for $50 and priced and sold it for $400.

16. Peanuts items are another great seller on eBay. Remember Charlie Brown, Lucy and Snoopy? Any item you can find that is Peanuts will sell quickly, this

includes, toys, coloring books that have not been used, bed sheets or blankets.

17. Vintage cookbooks always sell great as well. One in particular is the Betty Crocker cookbooks. You need to avoid the newer ones and the ones that focus on the microwave. If you can find old cookbooks that are in good condition you can usually pick these up for about $1 a piece and sell them for upwards of $20.

Those are the items for this chapter that you can find at thrift stores very easily and sell on eBay for a profit. My tip for this chapter is that you list often. If you only list one item a week your listings will get lost, when someone searches for the items you are selling the items that were posted the most recent will show up first. Make sure you keep your items in the top few search pages.

Chapter 3
What Else Should You Look For?

18. Blank cassette tapes are always a great find because you cannot go out to your local retail stores and find them anymore. There are still people who love using cassette tapes and will pay good money for them. I never purchase cassette tapes unless they are still sealed in the original packaging and you can make more money with them if you can sell them in lots. I recently was able to purchase 10 tapes for $5 total and sold them in a lot for $45. Look for the brands Denon and Maxell.

19. Just like blank cassette tapes, blank VHS tapes are a great find. Again this should be in their original packaging and it is great if you can purchase several over time and sell them as a lot. Since these are outdated media it is very hard for people to get their hands on them, so they are willing to pay quite a bit for them.

20. You should also keep an eye out for blood pressure machines. Now you are not going to get rich selling these, but you can easily make a $15 profit on a blood pressure machine that you paid $5 for. Always double check and make sure it works before purchasing.

21. I already talked about toys but you should really watch for Care Bears. These were very popular in the 80's and are very popular on eBay. If you look in the area where your thrift store keeps the stuffed animals, you can usually find these and purchase them for less than $1. List them on eBay and sell them for $20 or more.

22. Doll house furniture is another specific item you need to watch for. You can sell these piece by piece or you can create a lot of them if you find enough. Purchasing

$20 worth of doll house furniture can bring in a $200 profit without any problem. But don't just focus on the furniture, watch for doll house building items such as tiles or shingles. Many people collect these as well.

Don't purchase entire doll house kits unless you plan on breaking it up and know you can turn a profit. These are very heavy and cause issues when trying to ship them.

23. Another strange item that sells well on eBay is electric pencil sharpeners. Many people look for older models because they are better built than the ones that sell in stores today. If you can find an electric pencil sharpener, you can list it on eBay for $25 and it will sell quickly.

24. Back to the 80's era toys watch for Puff the Magic Dragon. These are rare but when you find them they usually cost less than $1 and sell for about $30. This is another item that sells quickly and you don't have to worry too much about packing it for shipping because there is nothing that will break on it.

25. Did you know that people are always looking for scrabble tiles? You can usually find these in a bag near the games and if you stock up on them you can make a decent amount from them. You can make about $10 for 100 tiles and many thrift stores will just save these for you and give them to you for free, who doesn't want to make a free 10 dollars?

26. Remember the time before there were MP3 players there was a wonderful item called a Walkman? Watch for these while you are out and about in your thrift stores. These are another hot selling item on eBay and you can usually get them for just a few dollars. Make sure they work and check the battery area to make sure

there is no corrosion or old batteries have not been left in it.

27. Old tube radios are a great item to sell as well and they show up so often in thrift stores. Some of these will sell for around $60, others will sell for thousands of dollars. I recently purchased one for $25 and sold it for $200. I had no clue what I was purchasing and had actually bought it for my house, after a bit of research I decided to sell it.

Before you list your items on eBay make sure you do a little bit of research about the item. Try to find out the year it was made, find out what the value of the item is before you list it so you do not lose money. Make sure you clean the item and take a great picture of it. If there is any damage you need to make sure to list that as well.

Chapter 4
Even More Items You Can Resell For Good Money

Before we begin this chapter I want to make a point. You don't need to go out and try to find all of these items all at once. Instead, choose one or two things that you will search for, then just keep your eye out for items that you think will sell. Always check your phone and see if they are selling on eBay. You can do this by searching the completed listings on eBay. If you go out and try to find all of these items you are just going to overwhelm yourself.

28. Ties are an item that you can usually find at most thrift stores and depending on the condition you can usually sell these for a good profit. Now you don't want to purchase your everyday ties, instead you want to watch for the odd ones. Ties that have characters on them like Taz or ties that have odd sayings, these are the ones that sell the fastest and for the most profit.

29. Most books will not sell well on eBay but there are a few that you should watch for. Little House on The Prairie books and Harry Potter books sell great. If you can find an entire collection you will be able to bring in an even larger profit. One thing I like to do is pick up a book here and there when I find them. Once the collection is complete you can sell them for a profit.

30. House décor is so cheap at thrift stores, in fact it is one place that I prefer to buy items to decorate with. This can be items such as flower pots or a center piece for a table, or even fake floral arrangements. You can purchase these for $1-$2 and sell them for at least $10. You do want to watch the weight of the items though

because most people do not want to pay more for shipping than they are for the item itself.

31. Knick Knacks are in abundance at thrift stores and sell for about a quarter a piece max. If you can purchase an entire collection of them and sell them as a lot you will make a huge profit. Spending just $2.50 can bring you a $20 profit with no problems.

32. Old Christmas lights are an item that many people overlook but can be sold on eBay for a profit! By old I do not mean 2 or 3 years old, I mean Christmas lights from the 50's or 60's. You can get about $40 for just one strand of these lights. Always check to make sure the lights are working before purchasing.

33. Cast iron skillets will bring in a huge profit as well. I recently found a set of four skillets for $7 at a local thrift store. I took them home, cleaned them up and sold the entire set for $134. These have to be vintage cast iron and you will have to know how to clean them up if you want to sell them. If you know how to clean and season cast iron there is a lot of money to be made.

34. Vintage cake decorating books will sell for a huge profit as well. You need to make sure they are in good condition but a $1 investment can bring you $45 in profit.

When you are in thrift stores looking for your items, shop like it is your job because it is. Don't look at this as a hobby because if you do you will not be successful. I am not saying that you should not take risks but you need to be careful in doing so.

Chapter 5
Unique Items You Never Thought Would Sell

35. Two colored golf balls are another item that seems strange but sells like crazy on eBay. I have seen some of these balls go for over $60 with an investment of only $1-$2.

36. While you are digging around the clothes in your thrift shop keep an eye out for square dancing items. Many of these will sell very quickly on eBay. Most of the time you can get a square dancing dress for $8 at a thrift store and sell it for $80 or more on eBay.

37. 8 track players!!! This is an item that I see all the time and can usually get for $5-$10 and sell for a couple hundred on eBay. You need to know a little bit about them so make sure you do your research before you purchase any. You need to make sure they work as well but these are an amazing find.

38. This brings me to my next item which is 8 tracks. Just like cassette tapes these are going to sell quickly and you can make a great profit off of them. Unlike cassette tapes you will need to pay attention to what is on the tracks. A random track of someone speaking is not going to sell you need to know a little bit about music to make this work.

39. You should also watch for old records and record players. You can find record players for about $10-$20 and sell them for close to $100 and you can find records for about $1 a piece. I like to keep a record collector guide with me while looking at records. This way I can quickly refer to the guide and know whether the record is going to be profitable or not.

40. Old bamboo fishing rods will bring in a great profit as well. It is amazing when you purchase an old fishing rod for a couple of dollars and turn around and sell it for $50-$150. Your profit will depend on the length of the rod and the condition of it but you can guarantee this will sell very quickly.

Once you have been going to thrift stores for a little while, don't be afraid to branch out a little bit and shop at flea markets or estate sales as well. Most of the items in this book can be found in these places just as easily as they are found in thrift stores and sometimes it is easier to find them at the flea market or estate sales. Just make sure you do not end up paying more for an item than you would at a thrift store. Keep your profit in mind during all of your purchases.

Chapter 6
Some 1980's Items You Can Sell and Make Profit On

41. Remember how popular My Little Pony was back in the 80's? Well guess what, it is just as popular now with a bit of a higher price tag. I have sold lots of 50 My Little Pony's for well over $200. This was about a $25 investment so anytime you see them make sure you grab them and put them away until you have a nice little stash.

42. Have you ever known that person who had an entire room full of Hot Wheels still in the package or Star Wars figurines? Well guess what, these people are willing to pay a ton of money for these and you can find them at thrift stores! Keep an eye out for anything that was made pre 90's and has the packaging in good condition.

43. Smurfs are another item you need to keep your eyes peeled for. It does not matter if what you find is the small plastic Smurfs, the stuffed ones or even if it is bed sheets. I sold one Smurfette bed set sell for over $50. The only thing you need to watch is that you are not trying to sell the new Smurfs as the old ones. Look at the tag and make sure otherwise you will have some very unhappy customers.

44. As you can see there is a lot of money in different types of toys, another item to watch for is old Winchester toy guns. Most of these are cap guns and can bring in up to $50 each depending on the condition of the gun.

45. Military items sell quickly as well, watch for anything from WW2 or earlier, helmets, uniforms literally everything sells.

Remember to watch for things you don't see often when you are shopping. Many people will see items such as a bread maker priced at $2 and think they can turn a huge profit, but look at how many bread makers are on the shelf. 5, 10 maybe 15 even. Watch for the rare, not the items you know the thrift store will have every time you go in.

Chapter 7

The Odd Selling Items That Sell Great

In this chapter I want to give you a few items that you can find literally everywhere and still make a profit from them on eBay. I am not going to pretend I know why these items sell, who buys these items or what use anyone has for these items. I am however going to warn you that these are quite strange but you can still make a profit off of them.

46. Pine cones. If you find a box of pine cones lying around a thrift store, you can list them on eBay and sell them for $30. Find an extra large pine cone and get $30 out of it all by itself. If you can't find these in a thrift store, grab a bag and start searching for them. Pine cones equal big money.

47. Vintage stickers can bring in some big time money. Look in your thrift store in the knick knack section. I once found a bag full of 1980's skateboard stickers for $5. They threw 100's of original 1980's skateboard stickers in 1 bag. I sold the same Vision Street Wear and Powell Peralta 1980's vintage skateboard stickers over and over for years at $10 a piece.

48. Altoids candy tins are another item people go crazy for. These do need to be vintage, but are super easy to find at thrift stores and most of the time they will just give them to you, but don't be fooled some of these sell for several hundred dollars each.

49. Vintage synthesizers. Always keep your eyes peeled for vintage synthesizers like the Moog and Roland Juno 106. Usually the thrift store does not know the difference from a cheap little Casio keyboard and a truly vintage synthesizer. Basically as a rule of thumb, the more knobs the synthesizer has, the better. I bought a Roland Juno 106 at a thrift store for $20 and resold it on eBay for over $500.

50. The last item I have for you is your egg cartons. When you buy a dozen eggs in those foam like cartons, save them farmers will purchase them from you, you can get about $10-$15 dollars for 40 of them and all you have to do is eat your eggs.

Those are the 50 items that you can purchase at a low cost and sell on eBay for a profit, but before I finish up this book I want to give you a few tips that you can use while you look for items.

First don't feel like you need to stick to what I have told you in this book. When I first started out, I would pick up an item and ask myself would I purchase this for myself, would anyone I know purchase it, if I could answer yes to either question and the item was cheap enough I got it.

You should also try to shop in high end areas. So many people would rather donate to thrift stores instead of having a yard sale or selling their items on eBay. If you want to get high end items you need to shop in thrift stores that are in high end areas. This is especially helpful when you are looking for name brand clothing or fur. One warning though, most of these thrift stores know their items are high end and will charge more than other thrift stores.

You need to make sure you take a few items with you. You should always have a smart phone. You also need to make sure you take a few batteries with you when you are shopping. If you are looking for a Walkman you need to take a cassette with you that you know works as well as a pair of headphones.

Keep some anti-bacterial lotion wipes with you as well, you are going to be going through a lot of items, many of these are dirty or dusty, and they have been handled by many other people. You will want to not only keep your hands clean but germ free as well.

Another tip is that you should get to know the people who work in the stores you shop at the most. This can be a huge asset. If you take a few minutes and get to know them, they tend to let you know if they have come across great donations.

Some will even call you and let you know something great has been put out on a shelf. Some will even hold items back for you!

Thrift stores have days where different items are on sale. Sometimes there may be a bag sale where you can purchase an entire bag of clothing for only a few dollars. Sometimes electronics will be on sale and so forth, you get the idea. These are the days you want to shop and really stock up on product. You can also shop at the end of season sales if you don't mind holding on to your product for a little while before turning a profit. This also requires some storage space as well so it is not for everyone.

Plan a schedule and stick to it! I can't stress this enough. If you really are serious about making money from flipping thrift shop items, you need to make a plan and stick to it. This means finding out which stores are your favorite and visiting them every week. Listing your items without procrastinating and shipping as soon as payments are approved.

You can make money by flipping thrift shop items on eBay, but it is going to take work. There are going to be times that you are going to fail. Some months you will make more sales than others and some months you may not see any profit at all but that does not mean you should give up. Instead learn from the experience, figure out what you are doing wrong and move on.

Shop early in the morning, most thrift shops restock overnight although some will stock the shelves on Monday so you should shop early in the week and early in the day. You will find the best items this way instead of having to choose what others have already picked through.

Have a system as well. Make a plan for going through each thrift store. For example, start with the clothing, then the shoes, electronics, move on going through each area of the store. Without a plan it can be very overwhelming and you will end up focusing on the stress instead of focusing on finding great items to sell.

I know the items in this last chapter were a little odd but I did that for a reason. The truth is almost anything will sell on eBay if you are willing to wait for the right buyer to come along. Sometimes this means your items will fly off of your shelves and other times it means the items will sit for a long time. However, if you focus on what I have told you in this book and use the tips I have given you, your items will sell quickly.

I hope that you enjoy flipping thrift store items!!! If you give the ideas I have taught you in this book a try, you will soon be raking in huge profits!

Conclusion

Thank you again for downloading this book!

I hope this book was able to help you to start learning how to flip thrift store items and sell them on eBay.

The next step is to head out to the thrift store and see what you can find.

Finally, if you enjoyed this book, then I'd like to ask you for a favor, would you be kind enough to leave a review for this book on Amazon? It'd be greatly appreciated!

Click here to leave a review for this book on Amazon!

Thank you and good luck!

Check Out My Other Books

Below you'll find some of my other popular books that are popular on Amazon and Kindle as well. Simply click on the links below to check them out. Alternatively, you can visit my author page on Amazon to see other work done by me.

http://www.amazon.com/Turning-Thrift-Store-Finds-Into-ebook/dp/B00S33XFXK

http://www.amazon.com/Thrift-Store-Reselling-Secrets-Wish-ebook/dp/B00U4HXQV4

http://www.amazon.com/Turning-Thrift-Store-Clothing-Into-ebook/dp/B00U4HXUME

http://www.amazon.com/eBay-Selling-Secrets-Massive-Profits-ebook/dp/B00TJMBJDM

http://www.amazon.com/Unlocking-eBay-Goldmine-Maintain-Profitable-ebook/dp/B00Q7O0Z1W

http://www.amazon.com/Unlocking-Etsy-Goldmine-Profitable-Business-ebook/dp/B00P35V5I8

Made in the USA
San Bernardino, CA
19 February 2020